COOL CAREERS WITHOUT COLLEGE
FOR PEOPLE WHO LOVE
CODING

ASHER POWELL

Rosen
YA
™
New York

Published in 2018 by The Rosen Publishing Group, Inc.
29 East 21st Street, New York, NY 10010

First Edition

Library of Congress Cataloging-in-Publication Data

Names: Powell, Asher, author.
Title: Cool careers without college for people who love coding / Asher Powell.
Description: New York City : The Rosen Publishing Group, 2018. | Series: New cool careers without college | Includes bibliographical references and index. | Audience: 7–12.
Identifiers: LCCN 2016059243 | ISBN 9781508175360 (library bound : alk. paper)
Subjects: LCSH: Computer security—Vocational guidance. | Coding theory—Vocational guidance. | Computer programming—Vocational guidance. | Artificial intelligence—Vocational guidance.
Classification: LCC QA76.9.A25 P677 2017 | DDC 005.1023—dc23
LC record available at https://lccn.loc.gov/2016059243

Manufactured in China

CONTENTS

With the high cost of a college education, students will want to look at all other options before having to take out a student loan. But our world is more fast-paced and competitive than ever before, and technology seems always to be changing. From tablets to computers to mobile phones, we're connected to the rest of the world. Just how connected? A 2015 study found that 64 percent of American adults own a smartphone, a huge leap from just 35 percent in 2011. And what are we doing on our phones? We're using them to learn and share with others. The same study found that 68 percent of smartphone users use their phone at least occasionally to follow breaking news events; 67 percent use their phones to share photos, videos, or commentary

A society connected by technology means jobs developing and maintaining technology are in demand. Could one of them be the right job for you?

about events; and 56 percent use their phones to learn about community activities and events.

This instant, mobile connection is important to us as a community. And there are people behind these devices—designing, building, coding, experimenting, and performing important jobs that few people think about when they download an app or take a picture.

A career in tech often doesn't need a college degree. While there are many colleges and institutions that offer coding degrees, certificates, and programs, often they aren't necessary. Companies are often looking for experience, not a formal education. With so many resources online, it's easy to learn without having to pay tuition. Online courses can provide week-by-week instruction. Nanodegrees are six- to twelve-month courses that teach basic coding skills at a low cost. Boot camps are ways to learn quickly in a short amount of time, and internships allow you to learn on the job. They're just some of the resources available as you learn not only how to code but what specific job you want to perform with your skills.

Because technology is a part of so much of our lives—from paying our bills on our phone to talking to a friend in another country—there is a wide variety of jobs that suit a wide variety of people. Are you artistic? You could go into design. Like to keep systems up to date? A system administrator job could be right for you. Do you have a clear vision and strong leadership skills? Product managers are always needed for keeping projects on course. New innovations come with new jobs, so the sky's the limit.

We can't cover every coding job available in this resource, so use this as a tool to give you an idea of specific areas of coding and the technology industry that are possible to explore. When you read about a career that interests you, use the For More Information sections as well as the internet to learn more about that career and other careers that focus on similar aspects of coding. As you go through the different careers, you'll see a common theme: networking, taking online courses and tutorials, and working on your own projects will take you far. Because of this, people with a lot of self-discipline who can work on projects without needing someone to manage them will be best suited for most of these careers. You will also see that as you progress through the resource, entry-level careers can lead to careers that require more experience. So while you may start as an iOS developer, you might use that to become a product manager one day.

CHAPTER 1

UX DESIGNER

Do you like color? Design? Art? The way an app looks when you open it? User experience designers, or UX designers, are the ones who are concerned with how the digital product looks and feels to the user. Every app you use—from messaging your friends to checking the weather before you go out to dinner—requires a UX designer.

UX designers focus on how the user interacts with the application or product and how the application is laid out on the screen. The goal is a product that not only performs its intended function but also feels easy to use and interact with.

User experience can be an artistic career. People who like being creative and coming up with lots of designs may enjoy creating the look of a product.

THE JOURNEY OF A USER INTERFACE

When designers first start out, they need to know what their objective is. How do they want to have a person interact with the product? What does this screen, or interface, need to look like? How does it need to function? Often this is a brainstorming session involving other team members, where a list of what the consumer needs from the product is generated.

From there, a designer might make sketches on paper to rough out what the interface might look like. After a rough sketch, a designer will go to the computer and build a wireframe, or a digital test of the design. There may be many wireframes; some can be just stationary mock-ups. Others will be interactive designs that can be tested and tweaked over and over again. These wireframes are constantly tested by users, and their feedback allows the designer to make changes to the interface. With each wireframe, the complexity grows. Designers need to be open to critique and be able to communicate at this stage.

The visual design comes next. Wireframes are given the final colors, typography, and added design elements to become mock-ups. Mock-ups should look and feel like they're ready to be used, but this is another stage of testing, critique, and reworking. Colors may need to be altered;

logos may need to go through several designs until the team settles on the right one.

With the mock-up done, a designer now moves to the next stage: usability testing. The product is continuously tested by users, and adjustments are made. These adjustments often happen even after the product is released, so the designer's job is isn't over. As more people use the application, more issues, or bugs, are found. So more fixes are made over the life of the application.

This is a booming, important part of the ever-expanding technology or tech scene, and it is often considered one of the most satisfying jobs to have due to flexible hours, competitive pay, and the ability to telecommute—better known as working from home. But the journey to a successful application design can be a long one. The competition can be fierce, and once working in the industry, UX designers have to have a tremendous amount of patience as they constantly build, test, and have their designs reviewed. A successful designer has to be able to understand some of a product's backend, as well as understand more art-based concepts and skills like color, design, and vector art. With so many different skills having to be utilized, and so many steps involved with creating a successful design, good project management and teamwork skills are a must. And as it becomes closer to a deadline, you may need to work under pressure and stay late to finish your work.

HOW TO BECOME A UX DESIGNER

Having an artistic side never hurts when you're starting out as a designer, but remember that you need some more skills under your belt than just an eye for composition. You're designing an interface that people will be interacting with, and the skills that you need to develop can only come from practice.

To design digitally, programs like Adobe Photoshop and Adobe Illustrator have long been the gold standard of a designer's digital toolkit. But with Adobe products now being expensive cloud-based applications with monthly subscription fees, other alternatives have been released. The Mac-based application Sketch is quickly becoming popular because of its versatility as a combination of both Photoshop and Illustrator and its inexpensive price point.

To learn how to use your digital tools, websites like Skillshare, Skillwise, LinkedIn's Lynda, and others are available to help. Videos can also be found on sites like YouTube. You can pay for as little or as much as you want for tutorials, classes, and help with learning. Books and ebooks on using these applications are also available.

UX designers need to constantly keep up with changing styles and techniques. It's important to read, study, and be inspired. Sites like LinkedIn and Medium host blogs by experienced designers who discuss topics ranging from how to break into UX design to the history of design and new emerging trends. Websites like the Best Designs and Dribbble house other UX designers' work, allowing you to gain inspiration and insight to how other designers work and present their finished products.

But the most important part of your self-education is practice. In order to be hired, designers need to constantly work on mock-ups of fake applications and products. Coming up with your own idea and creating a design around it allows you to showcase your skills without having to find a job first. You can present these designs to others and ask for critiques, and use them to develop a portfolio for interviewing for UX jobs.

PAY AND JOB PROSPECTS FOR UX DESIGNERS

Pay for UX designers is often a flat salary. Because most designers work for their company full-time, this is a negotiated amount that often includes benefits like health care, vacation, and sometimes traveling expenses. Salaries vary

Silicon Valley is the tech capital of the world. However, there are many coding jobs in other cities and towns in the United States. Some could even be close to you.

from state to state and country to country, with salaries being higher in areas that have high costs of living, like Silicon Valley. As you continue to grow and work, it's possible to receive raises and negotiate for a higher salary.

UX designers are in high demand, but competition can be fierce. Oftentimes it's easier to be brought into a company as an intern with the company hiring you full-time after the internship ends.

FOR MORE INFORMATION

ORGANIZATIONS

Center for Digital Media
 685 Great Northern Way
Vancouver, BC V5T 0C6
Canada
(778) 370-1001
Website: https://thecdm.ca
The Center for Digital Media is a cutting-edge school offering a master's program in digital media.

GrowthX Academy
44 Tehama Street
San Francisco, CA 94104
(415) 638-9161
Website: https://gxacademy.com
GrowthX Academy provides a twelve-week UX design program.

UX Club at UT Dallas
800 W Campbell Road
Richardson, TX 75080
Email: uxutdallas@gmail.com
Website: http://www.uxutd.com
The UX Club at University of Texas at Dallas.

BOOKS

Camara, Chad, and Yujia Zhao. *The UX Learner's Guidebook: A Ramp and Reference for Aspiring UX Designers.* Skokie, IL: Deuxtopia, Inc., 2015.

Unger, Russ, and Carolyn Chandler. *A Project Guide to UX Design: For User Experience Designers in the Field or in the Making.* 2nd ed. San Francisco, CA: New Riders, 2012.

BLOGS

Raska, Robin. "Great Books for Designers to Read in 2016." Design Pttrns, 2015. https://blog.pttrns.com/great-books-for-designers-to-read-in-2016-d2ebea3763f4#.vq7tby65j.

WEBSITES

Because of the changing nature of internet links, Rosen Publishing has developed an online list of websites related to the subject of this book. This site is updated regularly. Please use this link to access the list:

http://www.rosenlinks.com/CCWC/coding

CHAPTER 2

SYS ADMIN

System administrators, or sys admins, are in charge of making sure a computer system is maintained from within a company. They are a vital part of any organization, helping it to run smoothly and stay connected with customers, partners, and employees.

This is a job that can have a wide range of responsibilities, depending on the size of the company and its needs. Some companies may be smaller and have only a few computers and programs to be kept updated, while much larger—even international—companies have hundreds of employees and computers that

Companies depend on sys admins to keep their systems running and solve any issues that suddenly occur. Problem-solving skills are definitely needed!

need to be constantly kept up to date. Depending on the industry the company does business in, special software and hardware may be needed in order for the organization to perform optimally. Some sys admins may need to be familiar with certain routers, networking systems, and enterprise communication systems. You'll need to be someone who enjoys problem solving and helping others understand the technology they're using.

BUILDING, REPAIRING, REBOOTING

Sys admins need to have an understanding of multiple programs and the desire to learn new programs. Sys admins are constantly checking the security of the computer systems, running updates, and making sure everything is running optimally. As older programs are phased out and new ones are needed, they must install them onto the company's computers and make sure they run properly.

A sys admin may also be in charge of the organization's hardware. Any new equipment purchased may have to be cataloged and added to the inventory, and given any necessary software installations. Broken equipment may need repair, or entirely new equipment may need to be built from scratch.

One of the most important tasks sys admins perform is maintaining standards and practices for employees to use. When a new employee joins the company, sys admins set up a company computer and make sure the person has the correct programs, passwords, and access. They will often set up the company email and any other important applications on the employee's phone. They will explain the standards and practices and make sure the employee understands what is expected and how to use the company equipment and software. They may answer any questions a new employee may have about the system and help him or her learn how to navigate the company's intranet, or internal communications network. When an employee leaves, the sys admins in turn make sure all company equipment is returned and the employee's accounts are deleted.

Larger companies may require their own private software to manage certain tasks. A sys admin may help create this custom software and assist in building patches to fix issues.

BACKING EVERYTHING UP

Everyone knows how important it is to back up their documents. But when a company has hundreds of employees, how does everything get backed up?

DBAS, NETWORK ADMINS, AND SAN ADMINS

Sys admins have a lot of responsibility, but these roles can branch off into more specific titles within system administration. The larger the company, the more specific the jobs within administration can be as each person focuses on one area of a company's internal framework. As these roles take certain responsibilities from a more general system administrator, sys admins within these larger teams will find themselves directly in charge of the computer systems that are installed and operated on company hardware as these other roles focus elsewhere. To enter more specific roles, you may need to complete additional training and certifications.

A database administrator, or DBA, is in charge of the security and performance of a company's database. DBAs are constantly checking the efficiency of the database and maintain the database's security, which can be extremely important for organizations that handle confidential or private information, like hospitals, police stations, and schools. DBAs also keep database systems and handling programs up to date, as well as design and set up new databases. A DBA also needs to be able to train employees to be able to input and extract data through the various systems and applications used by the company or organization.

Network administrators are in charge of installing, configuring, and providing support to a company's networks. This includes a company's virtual private network (VPN), local area network (LAN), wide area network (WAN), and any routing and internet systems.

Storage area network administrators, or SAN admins, are directly in charge of a company's storage. A storage area network is a network dedicated specifically to a company's storage, where information is broken up and stored on multiple devices instead of in one place. This allows for the storage to operate at high speeds, and a SAN admin needs to be able to maintain this network's security and efficiency as well as trouble shoot any issues that may arise.

A sys admin needs to make sure this vital data is kept safe. A routine task is backing data up and making sure that there is enough space in a company's system to capture and store that data. For many companies, that space is in a commercial data storage service like Amazon Web Services. But in some instances, a company can have its own servers. Sys admins need to be comfortable with maintaining these servers and understand the physical requirements of a server when companies want to have their storage on site rather than in the cloud.

Data storage can go back years, allowing a company to keep detailed records of events for legal purposes. So the data that is stored needs to be easily searched and sorted. Sys admins who are highly detail-oriented will help their companies stay organized.

HOW TO BECOME A SYS ADMIN

Depending on the requirements being sought by a company, a sys admin can be well compensated. Some employers do look for a four-year degree in computer science, but often experience working in the field is just as valuable.

When you are just starting out, online resources are helpful and plentiful. Windows allows you to receive training for free, while open source systems like Linux have multiple guides published. Networking with other system administrators and reading about enterprise-level software and hardware can help you learn. Becoming

Free online courses are available to help you develop the skills you need in order to become a sys admin.

certified to maintain certain pieces of hardware and software can also make you a desirable candidate. Because there are so many different types of certifications for different operating systems and programs, it's best to decide what you're interested in learning before choosing any one certification program.

Your first couple of jobs may be small and more focused on home repairs for people who need IT assistance. But the more work you do, the more your résumé and experience will grow. Making contacts with other system administrators will help you know when potential jobs open up as well as give you people who can be your references.

FOR MORE INFORMATION

ORGANIZATIONS

League of Professional System Administrators (LOPSA)
1200 Route 22 East, Suite 200
Bridgewater, NJ 08807
(609) 219-6787
Website: https://lopsa.org
This is a nonprofit group that provides resources and
    support to sys admins around the world.

Network Professional Association (NPA)
3517 Camino Del Rio S, Suite 215
San Diego, CA 92108-4098
(888) NPA-NPA0
Website: http://www.npa.org
This is an organization for network
    computing professionals.

Usenix: The Advanced Computing Systems Association
2560 Ninth Street, Suite 215
Berkeley, CA 94710
(510) 528-8649
Website: https://www.usenix.org
This association provides a community for sys admins,
    engineers, computer scientists, and technicians.

BOOKS

Kralicek, Eric. *The Accidental SysAdmin Handbook: A Primer for Early Level IT Professionals.* New York, NY: Apress, Inc., 2016.

Limoncelli, Thomas A., Christina J. Hogan, and Strata R. Chalup. *The Practice of System and Network Administration: Volume 1: DevOps and Other Best Practices for Enterprise IT.* 3rd ed. Boston, MA: Addison-Wesley Professional, 2016.

White, Kevin M., and Gordon Davisson. *OS X Support Essentials 10.11: Supporting and Troubleshooting OS X El Capitan.* Berkeley, CA: Peachpit Press, 2016.

WEBSITES

Because of the changing nature of internet links, Rosen Publishing has developed an online list of websites related to the subject of this book. This site is updated regularly. Please use this link to access the list:

http://www.rosenlinks.com/CCWC/coding

CHAPTER 3

ANDROID/IOS DEVELOPER

With so many people using mobile devices, there's now an application, or app, for everything. From messaging your friends to paying your bills, planning your vacation, and even adjusting the temperature of your house or dimming the lights in your room, you can now do it all on your mobile device. As of June 2016, Apple's App Store surpassed two million apps. That's two million ways to organize, execute, and express what's happening in your life all from the comfort of your mobile device. We're a connected society, and we'll only continue growing this way.

Hundreds of apps need teams of developers to bring them from idea to product you can download on the app store.

A developer for either iOS or Android will find themselves in a large, fast-paced job industry with many types of projects that cater to every interest. Do you like working on finance applications? Messaging apps? Shopping apps? As a developer, you can choose what you're drawn to and focus on that category. There is a wide variety of applications, so if you like exploring and trying new projects, this could be for you.

Your education is easy to access as a developer. Android and Apple host their own courses and resources, giving developers immediate access to the tools and training they need to learn. Beyond the operating systems themselves, there are many courses, books, tutorials, nanodegrees, and blogs that provide a wealth of knowledge. Paying for training and education is unnecessary, but paid training can open up additional resources for you to use, so you may take it into consideration. Researching paid resources is important as they can be priced from a few dollars to several hundred and provide various types and amounts of training and information.

People who develop for iOS and Android are builders. They want to take a concept that solves a problem and use tools to turn that concept into a working product. They understand that mobile devices are constantly receiving software updates and that their product is never truly

APPLE OR ANDROID?

Some developers strive to learn both iOS and Android. Both operating systems account for 96.7 percent of the global market. But when you're starting out, it can be hard to decide which operating system, also known as an OS, to learn first.

The operating system for Apple mobile devices is iOS. This OS has much stricter criteria than Android. Because it's only available for Apple products, you can work only on iOS projects on Macbooks, as the tool set Xcode is Mac compatible only. For those who can't afford or make time to borrow a Mac, this can be a hurdle. Apple also requires developers to subscribe to a developer program, which allows them to submit apps to the app store. The subscription includes a yearly fee.

Android's development tool, Android Studio, is compatible with Mac, Linux, and Windows computers. But while Android beats iOS accessibility, Android Studio lacks some features and functionality that Xcode has available for developers, making it more difficult to create applications. While there is no subscription fee with Android, there is a one-time registration fee before you can submit an app.

Choosing what operating system to learn first is up to you, just remember each one has its pros and cons.

finished; it will constantly have to have patches, fixes, and upgrades to meet the demands of a phone or tablet's ever-changing OS. As developers, they're often one person on a team that is frequently collaborating and sharing ideas and critique. This might be the career for you if you enjoy teamwork and working closely with others.

FLEXING YOUR HACKATHON MUSCLE

Like many other careers, you can show off your talent at a hackathon for iOS or Android developers. Local hackathons can be found through your local developer communities and online meetup groups, and they are a

Meet fellow developers and practice your skills at hackathons, where you can compete for prizes, cash, and the ability to advance into bigger competitions.

great way to grow as a developer as they all start with a problem you must address. They allow you to flex your problem-solving skills and challenge yourself in ways you can't on your own. Judges will go over your final product, and you'll gain valuable feedback you can apply to your product or future products. The products you develop can then go in your portfolio and résumé, giving you new material to show potential employers.

You may not even have to seek out employers at a hackathon. People looking for developers to hire may see your project and approach you. For an employer, a hackathon is a good place to look at developers and see how they work under pressure as well as how they creatively solve a problem. Carry some business cards with you because you never know who will want to talk to you over lunch or via email.

If you win the hackathon, you may receive a large cash prize, hardware, and invitations to more prestigious hackathons. This allows you to continue to practice, earn money, and be visible to potential employers. The more prestigious and exclusive a hackathon is, the greater the prizes, exposure, and access to companies will be. This is why competing in hackathons and using them to improve your skills as a developer is an important exercise for you to use.

JOB OPPORTUNITIES AND PAY FOR A DEVELOPER

With so many apps not just in the app stores but in production waiting to be launched, iOS/Android developers with strong portfolios are in high demand. A typical salary will be on the higher end of the pay scale with room for raises as you grow in experience. But a developer's pay will vary wildly depending on whether or not the developer is a freelancer or a full-time employee. Remember, a freelancer does not have taxes deducted automatically, so while it may seem like a lot, be sure to set aside some of your earnings to pay your taxes at the beginning of the next year.

FOR MORE INFORMATION

ORGANIZATIONS

ACT: The App Association
1401 K Street NW, Suite 501
Washington, DC 20005
(202) 331-2130
Website: http://actonline.org
This association represents app companies and firms to fuel job creation and expand the application industry and mobile economy.

App Developers Alliance
1015 7th St NW
Washington, DC 20001
Email: Membership@AppAlliance.org
Website: http://www.appdevelopersalliance.org
This international association seeks to bring together developers and companies and be an advocate for application developers.

Mobile Developers of Berkeley
2360 Ellsworth Street, Apt. F
Berkeley, CA 94704
(425) 633-4156

Website: http://www.mobiledevsberkeley.org
This is a Berkeley-based community for
   mobile developers.

BOOKS

Eyal, Nir. *Hooked: How to Build Habit Forming Products.* New
   York, NY: Portfolio, 2014.
Keur, Christian. *IOS Programming: The Big Nerd Ranch Guide.*
   5th ed. Atlanta, GA: Big Nerd Ranch Guide, 2015.
Phillips, Bill. *Android Programming: The Big Nerd Ranch
   Guide.* 2nd ed. Atlanta, GA: Big Nerd Ranch Guide, 2015.

WEBSITES

Because of the changing nature of internet links, Rosen
Publishing has developed an online list of websites
related to the subject of this book. This site is updated
regularly. Please use this link to access the list:

http://www.rosenlinks.com/CCWC/coding

CHAPTER 4

FULL STACK DEVELOPER

A company needs a developer who knows the front end of a website as much as the back end. It needs someone who's fluent in most of the major programming languages and can bridge the gap between the front end development and the back end. A full stack developer is adept at working in many types of frames and working between the front end and back end of a product. Knowing the languages of both

Developers use programming languages to communicate instructions to a machine. Every action must be delivered specifically through programming.

front and back end allow a full stack developer to bridge the gap between the two. All front end developers should know some back end coding, and visa versa, but being fluent in both means a full stack developer can understand, create, and problem solve on both sides. If you have an attention to detail and you like problem solving, being a full stack developer might be for you.

FRONT END VS. BACK END

Which is which and what do they do?

The front end is also known as client-side development. This is the portion of the product that the customer interacts with. Not to be confused with UX design, the front end has more to do with the structure and the coding of the product, and less to do with the interface design. They do, however, often work alongside the UX designer, assisting with building and testing wireframes and mock-ups. They take the designs and work of the UX designer and translates them into code for the program to use, allowing the UX designer to test designs and discover which user interfaces actually work best for the application.

Front end developers know HTML, CSS, and Javascript, and are familiar with multiple frameworks. This is so a site can be versatile and scale to fit any device it's being viewed on, making it look nice and user-friendly, whether it's being accessed on a cell phone or a giant monitor.

Back end developers develop and build the systems that power the product. They're in charge of the back end: a server, database, and application that keeps everything running smoothly. Back end developers focus on creating clean code that is easy to manipulate and fulfills the needs of the project.

Back end developers need to know multiple languages, like Ruby on Rails, Python, Java, and PHP, to create and maintain their back end. PHP frameworks, tools like MySQL, and software like Git are also valuable to know as a back end developer.

DON'T BE A MASTER OF NONE

The desire to want to learn every language, tool, and software available to full stack developers can be strong. But trying to learn them all runs the risk of being spread too thin and not being particularly good at any one thing. Limit yourself to only a few skills and work on being the best at them in the beginning. The further you go in your career as a full stack engineer, the more opportunities you'll have to learn more and add to your résumé. Employers want a full stack developer who is fluent in the languages they know and able to create well-designed products with them. It's easy to want to be a jack-of-all-trades but even easier to be a master of none.

BECOMING A FULL STACK DEVELOPER

Full stack tutorials, classes, and programs are extremely popular online. Sites like Udacity, ibento, Fullstack Academy, and Fullstack. io have created multiple courses to learn from that start at the beginning level and progress to more advanced topics. College is rarely talked about for full stack development, so education toward your career will be found online.

Taking online boot camps and courses allows you to do something else that's important: network. Meeting other developers who are also trying to learn the same skills you are and making friends expands your knowledge as a developer. Other developers can assist with projects and help you grow by exchanging resources and potential employer information. Remember that

Other developers can give advice and help you solve problems that may pop up on a project build. But remember to also be helpful when people ask for your assistance.

people helping you should be helped in kind; share your own thoughts and resources. Learning development is less of a competition to get the next job as it is meeting, expanding, learning from, and helping your network.

Practice makes perfect for a full stack developer. The industry is interested in how much experience you have, so come up with your own projects, build your own products, launch them, and show others what you've built. Work on your friends' projects, learning and improving your skills together. Hackathons—competitions where design and development teams create products—are the perfect challenge to full stack developers. Many people form teams with their friends and enter these competitions. Prizes can be as small as a gift card and as large as thousands of dollars and invitations to even larger competitions. Winning a hackathon is an excellent accomplishment to add to a résumé and shows employers you have great problem-solving skills and can work in a very short time frame.

FULL STACK DEVELOPER PAY AND JOB PROSPECTS

Full stack developers are in high demand. Even if you haven't been previously hired, allowing potential employers to see your personal projects shows that you're serious about growing and learning as a developer. Interviewing with projects you've worked on, even for free, will only help you find the right developer job on the right team.

Salaries for full stack developers vary with the location where the company is located, but employees tend to make larger than average salaries for their work. You're expected to work longer hours to get big projects done on time, so if you don't mind working long hours, this might be the job for you.

FOR MORE INFORMATION

ORGANIZATIONS

Association for Computing Machinery
2 Penn Plaza, Suite 701
New York, NY 10121-0701
(800) 342-6626
Website: http://www.acm.org
This is the largest computing society and brings
together professionals, educators, and students and
connects them with communities and resources.

Software Engineering Institute
4500 Fifth Avenue
Pittsburgh, PA 15213-2612
(412) 268-5800
Website: https://www.sei.cmu.edu
This institute within Carnegie Mellon University focuses
on the education and advancement of software
engineers.

Usenix: The Advanced Computing Systems
Association
2560 Ninth Street, Suite 215
Berkeley, CA 94710

(510) 528-8649

Website: https://www.usenix.org

This association provides a community for sys admins, engineers, computer scientists, and technicians.

BOOKS

Bush, Eric. *Full-Stack JavaScript Development: Develop, Test and Deploy with MongoDB, Express, Angular and Node on AWS.* Nicholasville, KY: Red Sky Publishing, 2016.

Copeland, David B. Rails. *Angular, Postgres, and Bootstrap: Powerful, Effective, and Efficient Full-Stack Web Development.* Raleigh, NC: Pragmatic Bookshelf, 2016.

McDowell, Gayle Laakmann. *Cracking the Coding Interview: 189 Programming Questions and Solutions.* 6th ed. Palo Alto, CA: Careercup, 2015.

BLOGS

Fogarty, Tim. "Hackathons Are for Beginners." Medium, 2015. https://medium.com/@tfogo/hackathons-are-for-beginners-77a9c9c0e000#.h9c8io2np.

Khanra, Agradeep. "Beginner's Guide for Aspiring Full-Stack Developers in Today's Competitive World." LinkedIn, 2016. https://www.linkedin.com/pulse/beginners-guide-aspiring-full-stack-developers-todays-agradeep-khanra.

Suzuno, Melissa. "How I Went from Total Beginner to Senior Web Developer." Aftercollege, 2014. http://blog.aftercollege.com/went-total-beginner-senior-web-developer.

WEBSITES

Because of the changing nature of internet links, Rosen Publishing has developed an online list of websites related to the subject of this book. This site is updated regularly. Please use this link to access the list:

http://www.rosenlinks.com/CCWC/coding

CHAPTER 5

DATA SCIENTIST

Data is king. Each day, 2.5 quintillion bytes of data are produced, and companies are eager to understand it. Even though it's impossible to process it all, there's still a need to try to sift through all of this information and learn about people.

This is where data scientists, the rock stars of statistics, come in. Taking raw data and processing it with algorithms and math, data scientists find the stories and trends in the numbers. They help major retailers reduce costs and improve sales, energy utility companies predict usage patterns, and companies to focus their marketing campaigns, as well as assist in many other industries. A data scientist needs to be able to communicate these stories in terms that everyone else can understand, so if you're someone who enjoys taking complex ideas and information and translating them into simpler terms, this might be the job for you.

HOW TO BECOME A DATA SCIENTIST

Data scientists are in high demand right now, and because of that, the field commands high salaries. The highest of these salaries are six-figures or more and go to data scientists that have PhDs. However, you can begin a career as a data scientist without having to go to college.

One of the easiest but expensive routes to becoming a data scientist are online and in-person boot camps. These boot camps can ranger from being massive open door programs to highly competitive programs that students must apply to. Boot camps do, however, offer a complete step-by-step learning plan, a useful path to educating yourself about such a complex field. These

Nate Silver is a data scientist famous for his 2008 and 2012 presidential election predictions. He runs a statistical analysis website called fivethirtyeight.com.

boot camps tend to be more expensive than other forms of education, and some more advanced camps can cost over ten thousand dollars. So be careful when researching your education.

If boot camps aren't for you, or if you want to strengthen your knowledge before entering into a program, there are other ways to study. Someone interested in being a data scientist needs to be proficient in mathematics. Statistics and algebra are musts for a data scientist to study, but more advanced mathematics like calculus and logic need to be understood. Sites like Coursera and some colleges with online courses teach these subjects a la cart, allowing you to advance your mathematics learning without having to completely enroll into a traditional college.

Learning programming languages and frameworks is also important. Understanding coding languages like R, Python, or SQL and frameworks like Hadoop or Spark allows a data scientist to take large amounts of data and extract the relevant information, as well as build models on how the information acts in other scenarios.

This knowledge also helps a data scientist with learning and understanding machine learning. Machine learning is the ability for a computer to learn without being programmed to do so. For data scientists, machine

DATA SCIENTIST VS. DATA ANALYST

Data scientists and data analysts may sound similar, but they couldn't be more different. So how can you tell the difference?

A data analyst takes data and cleans, processes, and breaks it into small, digestible forms. Data analyzation is about the exploration of data.

A data scientist focuses on taking data and explaining the past, problem solving the present, and strategizing the future.

learning allows them to take a particular set of information and have the computer dive deeply into it, extracting data that lies deep within.

All of these more technical aspects—coding languages, frameworks, and machine learning—can be found online. There are free tutorials, exercises, and resources available for people looking to learn on their own. For someone interested in more structure, books, online courses, and nanodegrees are also available but at a cost.

THE COMPETITIVE DATA SCIENTIST

While developers have hackathons, data scientists have competitions of their own. Kaggle is a website for data scientists that gives people resources to learn data science, access to public data sets they can practice on, a job board, and open competitions. Competitions expose you to a wide range of problems to solve, giving you working experience with many issues you will face in your field. The strict time set for each competition teaches you to work quickly and efficiently, and you'll learn new techniques and ways to approach data.

Even though it is a competition, Kaggle allows forums where data scientists can solve problems together, giving you access to more experienced data scientists that can help you understand and learn. And as the competition ends, you'll gain instant feedback on how you did compared to the others, receiving a place and rank on Kaggle's leaderboard. The more competitions aspiring data scientists compete in, the more experience they gain and the better they become. Rising on the leaderboard and allowing your work to be seen can attract the attention of people looking for data scientists, which in the end can lead to work. It's an excellent resource for any data scientist at any experience level, giving you access to education as well as possible employers.

PAY AND JOB PROSPECTS FOR DATA SCIENTISTS

The demand for data scientists will not slow down anytime soon. Because they are so sought after, data

Data science jobs can allow some flexibility to work outside of the office. However, you have to be good at communicating with your teammates or clients.

scientists are paid high wages. However, anyone going into this field needs to ask themselves if the amount of studying and practice is worth working in this booming field. With so many different skills to master, you may find yourself studying and working for a long period of time before you are able to find a job, so finding alternative work while you learn how to become a data scientist should be factored in.

Once you are at the skill level where you can find work, your first jobs may not be full-time. Online freelance contract jobs are abundant, and some of these jobs can be seeking entry-level data scientists. If you're looking for more permanent employment, tech-friendly locations like the San Francisco Bay Area or Austin, Texas, may have more opportunities for full-time positions than other places, or you may find a company that allows you to telecommute, or work remotely from home.

FOR MORE INFORMATION

ORGANIZATIONS

American Statistical Association
732 North Washington Street
Alexandria, VA 22314-1943
(703) 684-1221
Website: http://www.amstat.org
Founded in 1839, ASA is the world's largest community
  of statisticians. ASA supports the development,
  application, and dissemination of statistical science.

Association for Computing Machinery
2 Penn Plaza, Suite 701
New York, NY 10121-0701
(800) 342-6626
Website: http://www.acm.org
This large computing society brings together
  professionals, educators, and students and connects
  them with communities and resources.

Data Science Association
7550 East 53rd Place, Unit 172622
Denver, CO 80217-2622
Website: http://www.datascienceassn.org

This nonprofit group supplies resources, education, and certification to those interested in pursuing data science.

BOOKS

Grus, Joel. *Data Science from Scratch: First Principles with Python.* Sebastopol, CA: O'Reilly Media, 2015.

O'Neil, Cathy. *Doing Data Science: Straight Talk from the Frontline.* Sebastopol, CA: O'Reilly Media, 2013.

Provost, Foster, and Tom Fawcett. *Data Science for Business: What You Need to Know About Data Mining and Data-Analytic Thinking.* Sebastopol, CA: O'Reilly Media, 2013.

BLOGS

Delgado, Rick. "How to Become a Data Scientist Without a Degree." Techvibes, 2016. https://techvibes. com/2016/02/22/how-to-become-a-data-scientist-without-a-degree-2016-02-22.

Import.io. "Data Scientists Vs. Data Analysts: Why the Distinction Matters." 2016. https://www.import. io/post/data-scientists-vs-data-analysts-why-the-distinction-matters.

Levine, Daniel. "How to Become a Data Scientist Without a Degree." Stitch, 2015. https://blog.stitchdata.com/5-things-you-should-know-before-getting-a-degree-in-data-science-40cddf44aac3#.ym5kxyy72.

WEBSITES

Because of the changing nature of internet links, Rosen Publishing has developed an online list of websites related to the subject of this book. This site is updated regularly. Please use this link to access the list:

http://www.rosenlinks.com/CCWC/coding

CHAPTER 6

GAME DEVELOPER

In 2015, gaming became a $23.5 billion industry. Console games, online games, and mobile games alike are all enjoyed by millions of people. More than ever, the industry is looking for programmers and coders who can help bring games to the market. And with platforms like Steam, it's become easy to build, publish, and distribute your own games.

Part of the video game industry's popularity lies within its wide variety. Now games are no longer just played on a video game console or handheld gaming device, but on phones and tablets. There are games for Mac, Android, Facebook, and other online sites. With so many options, there are just as many different

With lots of studying and hard work, a love of video games can transform into a career where you help create them.

coding languages and platforms for you to learn. So make sure that you do some research before deciding on what type of developer you'd like to be.

Many different schools offer programs for game development, but these programs often come with high costs. Like other type of companies we've looked at, a game company is looking more for experience than a degree. There are a variety of online courses and tutorials available to learn various coding languages and platforms. Once you know what kinds of games you'd like to develop, enroll in the right course or courses for you. If there are other students, make sure to talk to them and connect. The game industry, like so many of our other careers, runs on networking. Friends are invaluable; you can talk through problems, help each other with projects, and refer one another for job openings.

As you learn more programs, make sure to use these new skills to create new games. As a game developer, your portfolio will help you find work, so you want to have projects available to show how much you know and can do. Work on other people's projects and make sure to take internships when possible.

BEWARE OF CRUNCH TIME

Video games have to be out on time, so when a game nears its release date, the team working on it often go into what the industry calls "crunch time." This form of overtime often does

Crunch time can mean spending weekends at the office with your team in order to finish building a game on time.

not have overtime pay, but it will have one thing: long hours. Some days during a crunch can be over twelve hours, with six days working and only one day off. It's a stressful, tiring period for a team releasing a game.

The video game industry has recently come under fire for the practice of crunch because of the extreme strain on workers. Always be aware that if you work in the video game industry, you'll most likely have to go through a crunch time and that long hours paired with little sleep can and will affect your physical and mental health. There are numerous articles

VIRTUAL REALITY AND OCULUS RIFT

In 2012, the future came in the form of a Kickstarter campaign. The Oculus Rift was the first virtual reality headset to be affordable enough for the everyday gamer, and it promised a completely immersive experience for campaign backers. The Kickstarter was quickly funded, and the company, Oculus, became immensely popular. Virtual reality, a technology often remembered as an awkwardly large pair of goggles and gloves and crude graphics during the late 80s, was suddenly being explored by companies like Google.

But while the Rift was supposed to be for gamers, virtual reality has quickly become considered the future for other industries. The immersive experience of virtual reality, or VR, makes it useful in many different ways. Designers have already found ways to use VR to create 3D to-scale designs of houses and various infrastructures that they can walk through and examine closely in VR before even building. Video conferencing could soon bring everyone in a meeting from different parts of the world all together in one place. Teachers could one day have students use headsets to interact with simulated events and scenarios, allowing them to experience a part of history or solve a complex problem. And for doctors, VR and scanning technologies could be a window to look inside a patient's body before they even perform surgery.

Time will tell how we use VR in non-gaming industries. But for someone looking to work with a particular piece of technology that has many possible uses in a variety of different industries, this might be for you.

online chronicling the problem of crunch in the industry and the effect is has on people and their families that are worth reading to understand how difficult working in the video game industry can be. This job may not be for you if you value flexible hours and the ability to take time off.

PAY AND JOB PROSPECTS FOR GAME DEVELOPERS

The video game industry is booming. Due to many people's desire to work in video games, it may take awhile to get your foot in the door. With so many people applying for the same

Every year companies announce and unveil the new games they are developing to the public at GDC, or the Game Developers Conference.

position, you have to have a portfolio and résumé that stand out. At many companies, it can sometimes be a matter of who you know who can recommend you for the job, which ties back into a game developer's need to network and make friends with fellow developers and artists. Attending conferences like the Game Developers Conference, or GDC, can also be beneficial as many companies have booths and are open to portfolio reviews.

The pay for a game developer is generally good and allows a developer to live a comfortable life. The actual amount depends on a number of factors. Some developers are full-time while others can be just contract-based and the work for hire. While contract work may initially seem to pay more, be aware that you have to pay your own taxes with freelance work and that you need to set some of your payment aside to have enough money to do so come tax season.

FOR MORE INFORMATION

ORGANIZATIONS

Game Dev Club at SJSU
1 Washington Square
San Jose, CA 95192
Website: https://sjsugamedev.com
This club at San Jose State University explores
    game development.

International Game Developers Organization
19 Mantua Road
Mt. Royal, NJ 08061
Website: https://www.igda.org
This nonprofit organization is dedicated to the
    education and nurturing of future game developers.

Museum of Art and Digital Entertainment
 3400 Broadway
Oakland, CA 9461
(510) 210-0291
Website: https://themade.org/?nav
This museum is dedicated to digital entertainment,
    including video games. The museum puts on
    classes and hosts meetups around video games and
    game development.

BOOKS

Cho, James S. *The Beginner's Guide to Android Game Development.* Dublin, Ireland: Glasnevin Publishing, 2014.

Chopra, Samanyu. *IOS Game Development by Example.* Birmingham, UK: Packt Publishing, 2015.

Manning, Jon, and Paris Buttfield-Addison. *Mobile Game Development with Unity: Build Once, Deploy Anywhere.* Sebastopol, CA: O'Reilly Media, 2017.

BLOGS

Rubin, Peter. "The Inside Story of Oculus Rift and How Virtual Reailty Became Reality." Wired, 2014. https://www.wired.com/2014/05/oculus-rift-4.

Schreier, Jason. "The Horrible World of Video Game Crunch " Kotaku, 2015. http://kotaku.com/crunch-time-why-game-developers-work-such-insane-hours-1704744577.

Tambay, Guatam. "The Best Free Online Resources to Learn Game Development and Gamification." Springboard, 2014. https://www.springboard.com/blog/free-online-courses-game-development-gamification.

The Verge. "The Rise and Fall and Rise of Virtual Reality." Retrieved 2016. http://www.theverge.com/a/virtual-reality.

WEBSITES

Because of the changing nature of internet links, Rosen Publishing has developed an online list of websites related to the subject of this book. This site is updated regularly. Please use this link to access the list:

http://www.rosenlinks.com/CCWC/coding

CHAPTER 7

QA ENGINEER

Someone has to make sure the product you're building is up to snuff. A quality assurance engineer, or QA engineer, follows the product throughout all of its phases and has a deep understanding of programs as well as the desire to learn new ones. The job of a QA engineer is to oversee from start to finish that the product maintains the high quality the team is striving for and that it arrives on time and on budget.

QA engineers are involved with many aspects of a product's development. They will help write and review code, help with design and integration, and oversee management processes.

Quality assurance engineers must pay strong attention to details as well as be able to multitask and juggle multiple parts of a project with ease.

In the end, they will test the product rigorously, searching for bugs and glitches, and pushing the product to its breaking point. They must make sure that the product meets all company and government guidelines and that in the end it also fits the needs of the customer. When a project is running late, a QA engineer often stays later with the team, making sure deadlines are met. Often,

GOOD COMMUNICATION

With so many different teams, stages, and goals to keep track of, communication is key. A good QA engineer understands that in order to make sure everything runs smoothly, teams need to be unified and aware of what is going on outside of their roles. Developing a good communication infrastructure is important, as is knowing how to communicate and check in on people and teams in a business environment.

A QA engineer will want to make sure everyone understands their role within the project as well as make sure everyone knows how to communicate with their QA as well as other teams. Setting up weekly, biweekly, or monthly progress meetings is also key. These allow the entire team to get an overview of what stage the project is in and whether or not it's hitting its goals. These progress meetings can be as simple as an in-office meeting or as complex as a video-call with employees from all over the globe.

resources may be running short, and a QA will have to come up with creative solutions for the restraints the project comes up against.

With so many roles and steps to keep track of, QA engineers need to be master planners. They need to break down everything into smaller, more manageable goals that can be met, giving each stage and task a different deadline. This allows them to keep track of the entire process and assures that the product will hit its final deadline. Because of the need to constantly keep track of so many details and stages, being a QA engineer may suit someone who is organized, has an attention to detail, and enjoys organizing large projects. It may not be suitable for those who prefer to work without any kind of schedule.

HOW TO BECOME A QA ENGINEER

Because a QA engineer has so many different responsibilities, the path to becoming one is less about learning through instruction and more about learning through experience. While you can seek out degrees in quality assurance, studying books and online resources allows you to develop hands-on training. QA engineers should already have some experience in coding languages and frameworks. Ideally, they've already worked on other projects as an engineer, so other careers in this book may prove to be stepping stones on the path to becoming a QA engineer.

Working on other products also allows you to gain experience working with others as well as seeing all of the stages of a product's development. As an aspiring QA designer, you can develop an understanding of what a product needs and how things should be broken up and managed. Consider becoming an iOS or Android developer, a UX designer, or any other one of the careers that touch products during development. Remember to take the time to weigh the pros and cons of each career and what type of products you would eventually like to be a QA engineer for.

QA engineers should also study testing, as it's an important part of their role. There are many books and online resources for testing, like the website uTest, that give people interested in testing forums, tutorials, articles, and even classes and certifications. Learning how to test a product can also lead you to being able to apply to be a tester. While being employed as a tester does not pay as much as a QA engineer, it can be a job that provides a steady income while studying to become a QA engineer.

QA engineers may also want to study communication. When working with so many different people, they need to be able to speak clearly and concisely with others, work well under pressure, and be able to explain what goals or issues the product may be facing. Being able to compose well-

You'll never be working by yourself as a QA engineer. You need to be able to communicate clearly to many different people working on the project.

written, professional emails and reports is an important skill to have, so someone looking into becoming a QA designer may want to take the time to pracice their writing skills.

PAY AND JOB PROSPECTS FOR QA ENGINEERS

We're a country that is constantly innovating and developing new products. Because of this, companies need QA engineers in order to keep projects running on time so they can be delivered to consumers. QA designers are needed wherever technology is being designed, so certain cities will need QA engineers more than others. Expect to be paid well, with the ability to earn more as you gain more experience.

Because this is a career where you need to not only learn many skills but also work in another career before making a transition into being a QA engineer, take the time to consider if this career is right for you. You will have to have the patience to learn, work, and develop the skills you need, which can take several years.

FOR MORE INFORMATION

ORGANIZATIONS

Computer History Museum
1401 N Shoreline Boulevard
Mountain View, CA 94043
(650) 810-1010
Website: http://www.computerhistory.org
This nonprofit museum preserves the history and
impact of computing on the world.

IEEE Computer Society
2001 L Street NW, Suite 700
Washington, DC 20036-4928
(202) 371-0101
Website: https://www.computer.org/web/guest
IEEE Computer Society provides resources, conferences,
journals, and a digital library for those interested in
computer science and technology.

Usenix: The Advanced Computing Systems Association
2560 Ninth Street, Suite 215
Berkeley, CA 94710
(510) 528-8649
Website: https://www.usenix.org

This association provides a community for sys admins, engineers, computer scientists, and technicians.

BOOKS

Crispin, Lisa, and Janet Gregory. *More Agile Testing: Learning Journeys for the Whole Team.* Boston, MA: Addison-Wesley Professional, 2014.

Pyzdek, Thomas, and Paul Keller. *The Handbook for Quality Management, Second Edition: A Complete Guide to Operational Excellence.* New York, NY: McGraw-Hill Education, 2013.

Tech, Solis. *Quality Assurance: Software Quality Assurance Made Easy.* Charleston, SC: CreateSpace Independent Publishing Platform, 2016.

WEBSITES

Because of the changing nature of internet links, Rosen Publishing has developed an online list of websites related to the subject of this book. This site is updated regularly. Please use this link to access the list:

http://www.rosenlinks.com/CCWC/coding

CHAPTER 8

DEVOPS DEVELOPER

Communication between IT and development doesn't always happen. With so many stages in a product's development, roles and teams can become "siloed," or isolated from one another. Because of this lack of communication, the project or product may struggle to come together. The project's production speed may slow and become inefficient. Enter development operations, or DevOps. DevOps is a culture of philosophies and best practices that revolves around breaking down these silos and creating tools that speed up the process of product development. The goals of DevOps are optimization, or making things run at peak efficiency; rapid delivery, or the ability to release new features or fix bugs quickly; reliability; scalability, also known as the ability for a product to take on a bigger workload; collaboration; and security.

People who enter DevOps are people who are best at juggling many tasks at the same time. Because their goal is to increase optimization, they have to be able to work and address many problems a project faces. Developers build

Donovan Brown is a senior development manager for Microsoft. He spoke at the Microsoft Developers Build Conference in San Francisco, California.

tools that help achieve the six goals, collaborate with others, manage data, help with testing and deployment, and work across team borders. DevOps engineers are focused on the business outcomes of the project and helping the project reach its goal quickly. They are problem solvers who focus on how they can make things run quickly and smoothly, and they can work well with multiple groups of people. They can code and script, and enjoy learning about new cutting-edge tools and technologies.

HOW TO BECOME A DEVOPS DEVELOPER

Becoming a DevOps developer is similar to becoming a QA engineer. This is a career that does not require a degree, but it does require previous working experience before you're able to enter it. A DevOps developer needs to know many skills, including some IT operations, have an understanding of coding in at least one language, and have the ability to use and build tools. Because of this, it may be easier to learn another career that touches product development and expand your knowledge as you work within another role. There are many books, tutorials, and online resources for someone interested in a DevOps career and many people online that are available to give advice. Reading about and learning new systems and coding languages, as well as how to work with many tools and open-source software development products, are essential steps.

Someone who wants to work in DevOps should seek out projects that others are creating that need someone in a DevOps role. Working with other people on projects, much like other engineer and developer jobs, allows you to develop the professional skills you need in the DevOps field. Once completed, these projects can go on your résumé or in your portfolio, allowing you to use them as examples of work you've done when interviewing for DevOps jobs and to explain the different processes you used in order to get results. This is why networking within tech, through online sites and in-person meetups, continues to be important. You don't know if the next person you meet may be your future team member.

TOOLS, TOOLS, AND MORE TOOLS

A DevOps developer is expected to know how to use many different types of tools. These tools are often free to download and use, which makes the process of learning and understanding multiple tools easier. Some tools can be as simple as messaging platforms that allow greater communication across a project, while others can be more complex and assist in developing, testing, and delivering software.

Sometimes developers come across a problem they must solve where there isn't a tool readily available to download, and they may find themselves creating their own tools. Pain points, or problems, may be specific and unique to your project and no one else has experienced them. Problems can even be specific to individual teams and the stage of the build they are working on. You'll be called upon to use your problem-solving skills and creativity with code to develop tools to address these issues. And if you can't create a tool yourself, you'll need to reach out and collaborate with others on your project who can help you problem solve and create the tool you need.

Automation tools are one of the more important tools that DevOps developers needs to have in their digital tool-belt. These tools allow for testing of software applications at any time, repeatedly, without a DevOps developer having to be present. These tests are rapid, with each outcome stored and compared to the last one. This allows developers to be able to review the data from these multiple tests quickly and efficiently. With this data, they can make the proper adjustments to the software, improving the quality and fixing bugs. Automation tools cut down on time and work, and companies look for DevOps developers who know how to use them on projects.

DEVOPS DEVELOPER PAY AND PROSPECTS

DevOps is the role that originated from some of the biggest, most successful companies in Silicon Valley. Companies like Amazon, Google, and Facebook were the first companies to embrace the DevOps philosophies. Because more well-known companies praise this field, DevOps has spread throughout the tech industry. Companies are eager to streamline and optimize their production process, so DevOps developers can find themselves in demand. Salaries for DevOps developers are competitive, and in areas like Silicon Valley, developers can find themselves making well above the national minimum wage.

Because this field is similar to QA engineering, people interested in DevOps needs to ask themselves if the

The biggest companies in tech need skilled, experienced DevOps developers working for them in order to keep their sites running smoothly.

hard work developing multiple skills and the time spent working in another field is worth pursuing this field. You'll need discipline, focus, and patience to succeed in becoming a DevOps developer, so this job may not be for everyone.

FOR MORE INFORMATION

ORGANIZATIONS

BSA
20 F Street NW, Suite 800
Washington, DC 20001
(202) 872-5500
Website: http://www.bsa.org
This association is a global advocate for the
   software industry.

IEEE Computer Society
2001 L Street NW, Suite 700
Washington, DC 20036-4928
(202) 371-0101
Website: https://www.computer.org/web/guest
IEEE Computer Society provides resources, conferences,
   journals, and a digital library for those interested in
   computer science and technology.

Software & Information Industry Association (SIIA)
1090 Vermont Avenue NW, Sixth Floor
Washington, DC 20005-4905
Website: https://www.siia.net
(202) 289-7442

This is a trade association for software and digital content industries.

BOOKS

Kim, Gene. *The Phoenix Project: A Novel About IT, DevOps, and Helping Your Business Win.* Portland, OR: IT Revolution Press, 2014.

Kim, Gene, Jez Humble, Patrick Debois, John Willis, and John Allspaw. *The DevOps Handbook: How to Create World-Class Agility, Reliability, and Security in Technology Organizations.* Portland, OR: IT Revolution Press, 2016.

Warnock, Dan. *DevOps: From Newbie to Professional. Fast and Simple Guide to DevOps.* Charleston, SC: CreateSpace Independent Publishing Platform, 2016.

BLOGS

Bradford, Lawrence. "13 High Paying Tech Careers You Can Get Without a College Degree." Forbes, 2016. http://www.forbes.com/sites/laurencebradford/2016/07/06/13-high-paying-tech-careers-you-can-get-without-a-college-degree/#7c1faf1025bd.

Fisher, Anne. "Wanted: Highly Skilled Tech Workers, $100,000-Plus Salary, No College Required." Fortune, 2015. http://fortune.com/2015/05/13/devops-jobs.

Patrizio, Andy. "DevOps Tools: 20 Top Tools for Successful DevOps." Datamation, 2016. http://www.datamation.com/applications/devops-tools-20-top-tools-for-successful-devops-1.html.

Reynolds, Phillip. "I Want to Be DevOps!" Brassy, 2015. http://brassy.net/articles/getting-in-to-devops.

WEBSITES

Because of the changing nature of internet links, Rosen Publishing has developed an online list of websites related to the subject of this book. This site is updated regularly. Please use this link to access the list:

http://www.rosenlinks.com/CCWC/coding

CHAPTER 9

ARTIFICIAL INTELLIGENCE DEVELOPER

Artificial intelligence, or AI, has been described as the new heart of Silicon Valley. While we often think of the complex robots with human-like features of science fiction movies, current AI has a long ways to go before reaching those levels of complexity. Artificial intelligence currently performs functions that most people would consider simple but are often complex actions we take for granted as people, like understanding our internet surfing habits and suggesting pages. With each small step, though, AI gets closer to performing more complicated jobs like driving without a human at the steering wheel, following and assisting soldiers in battle, or helping the elderly. A cutting-edge, broad field, AI covers everything from computers translating text, to computers performing customer service, and Google and Tesla's new self-driving cars.

Machine learning is powering the self-driving cars that Elon Musk and his company Tesla Motors envision as the future of transportation.

MACHINE LEARNING AND NEURAL NETWORKS

Two of the biggest areas of artificial intelligence today are machine learning and neural networks. Machine learning, as we've discussed before, is the ability for a computer to learn without being programmed to do so. The machine goes through many, many tests, and each time takes the information that was the outcome and analyzes it to apply and adjust its own programming. This can be something as simple as your phone learning slang when you text and not flagging it with autocorrect the next time you send a message, to Facebook suggesting new friends, to auton-

SELF-DRIVING CARS AND THE FUTURE OF THE ROAD

One of the most exciting and talked about technologies today is an artificial intelligence that will soon have a major effect on our lives and commute times. Self-driving cars are

The Tesla Motors Model S car is equipped with autopilot technology that enables automatic lane changes and the ability to parallel park for the driver. It's a step closer to self-driving cars.

autonomous vehicles that can drive without the help of a human behind the wheel. They use GPS, sensors, an internal navigation system, and artificial intelligence to drive by themselves from one location to the next.

Currently self-driving cars are limited in their capabilities and can't drive a person to work or the grocery store just yet. However, millions of self-driving cars are predicted to be on

the road as soon as the year 2020. This technology will not only make your trips easier, but it will also provide transportation access for people who can't drive themselves, like the elderly and the disabled. Self-driving cars also mean fewer car wrecks, as the cars won't speed, drive too slow, or drive too close—common bad habits people have that lead to accidents.

With an increase in safety and more accessibility and mobility for people who can't drive, the self-driving car industry is one of the many possible fields someone interested in artificial intelligence can work toward being hired in. As self-driving cars hit the road and more are produced, automotive companies will be looking for AI developers and other engineers who can help create and improve self-driving cars.

omous robots exploring the surface of an asteroid without a scientist directing them.

Neural network is a certain type of machine learning that exists in a subgroup called deep learning. A neural network is software or hardware system that is designed to mimic the neural network of the brain. It is built to have a large number of processors that are in a tiered structure, with each tier feeding into the next. This means when data is entered, it goes through each tier step by step, exiting the final tier with its outcome. This allows the AI to be adaptable, and it is often used for pattern recognition applications. Current uses for neural networks are predicting patterns in the stock market, recognizing your handwriting when you write a check, and performing more complex actions like having robots recognize your face.

HOW TO BECOME AN ARTIFICIAL INTELLIGENCE DEVELOPER

Some people think that in order to work in artificial intelligence, you need to have a PhD. However, advanced degrees or even college isn't necessarily needed. You will, however, have to build upon other skills and knowledge. Understanding some coding languages like Python and R, and how to process and read data is important, as your job with AI will be building programs that can process data and learn by themselves. Working as a data scientist can be a smart first career on a person's way toward working with artificial intelligence. Because a data scientist must be familiar with machine learning, you can build on your education as you work in that field, learning more about deep learning and neural networks as you discover what you may want to do within the field of artificial intelligence.

Artificial intelligence can be a career that is built off of other careers and skills you've gained. Microsoft's Cortana writing team is made up of many experts from different fields.

Artificial intelligence is a popular technology, which means online resources are readily available for someone to learn. Blog, videos, and tutorials are great ways to learn. Kaggle, a data science website listed in another section, is a perfect place to practice machine learning problems with its competitions and public datasets. Competitions allow you to not only show your work but also to network with other people interested in artificial intelligence and be exposed to potential projects and employers.

PAY AND PROSPECTS FOR AN ARTIFICIAL INTELLIGENCE DEVELOPER

Artificial intelligence is a field that has taken the technology industry by storm. There are many uses for AI. From video games to finances to the auto industry to apps on smartphones, there are a wide variety of career choices for an AI developer. People interested in working with artificial intelligence should look at its various uses in different industries and see what career interests them the most. With so many options and skill levels needed, AI developers are in high demand and can be paid a wide range of salaries. Developers typically make good salaries with company benefits when they are hired full time. As you excel and gain more experience, advancement and pay raises are possible.

Because this is a career that is built upon prior experience, someone interested in being an artificial intelligence developer should consider the time and the dedication it takes to learn the skills necessary to work in this field. AI jobs may also be more plentiful in certain parts of the country, so thinking about possibly moving to pursue your career is important.

FOR MORE INFORMATION

ORGANIZATIONS

Association for Computing Machinery
2 Penn Plaza, Suite 701
New York, NY 10121-0701
(800) 342-6626
Website: http://www.acm.org
This computing society brings together professionals,
    educators, and students and connects them with
    communities and resources.

Association for the Advancement of Artificial Intelligence
2275 East Bayshore Road, Suite 160
Palo Alto, CA 94303
(650) 859-2000
Website: http://www.aaai.org
This nonprofit organization focuses on the
    advancement and understanding of the mechanisms
    underlying thought and intelligent behavior.

International Neural Network Society (INNS)
1123 Comanche Path
Bandera, TX 78003-421
(830) 796-9393
Website: http://www.inns.org

This is an organization for the theoretical and computational understanding of the brain and applying that knowledge to develop new and more effective forms of machine intelligence.

BOOKS

Conway, Drew, and John Myles White. *Machine Learning for Hackers: Case Studies and Algorithms to Get You Started.* Sebastopol, CA: O'Reilly Media, 2012.

Lantz, Brett. *Machine Learning with R.* Birmingham, UK: Packt Publishing, 2015.

Raschka, Sebastian. *Python Machine Learning.* Birmingham, UK: Packt Publishing, 2015.

WEBSITES

Because of the changing nature of internet links, Rosen Publishing has developed an online list of websites related to the subject of this book. This site is updated regularly. Please use this link to access the list:

http://www.rosenlinks.com/CCWC/coding

CHAPTER 10

CRYPTOCURRENCY DEVELOPER

When Bitcoin came onto the scene in 2008, it put cryptocurrencies on the map. Whether you want to work for a cryptocurrency—or build your own cryptocurrency—this industry will become more vital as we use more and more digital transactions.

Cryptocurrencies are important to digital transactions because they are incredibly safe compared to other digital forms of currency. As we shop more and more online, our credit cards and banking information are increasingly vulnerable to hackers. Large scale hacking scandals can take the personal information of thousands of people, putting their money and identities at risk. This risk is minimized by cryptocurrencies because they are decentralized, meaning the information is spread out among all

Bitcoin took the tech industry by storm and is now one of the biggest cryptocurrencies available. Are you interested in some of the newest technology emerging today?

of the users instead of kept in one location. This decentralized form of financial transactions is called blockchain, and it's often considered one of the most important technological discoveries of our time, only second to the internet itself.

The transaction information of a blockchain is kept on a ledger. There is not just one copy of the ledger but instead multiple copies that are spread out across a network and kept on points called nodes. When a transaction is made, it's recorded on this ledger, meaning there are multiple identical copies of the transaction. When the ledger is full, it is formed into what is called a block, which is secured by an encrypted code. Each block is connected to the block before it, so your current transactions are linked to the very first transactions ever made on the currency. This is what creates the chain of blocks the system is known for.

But what makes this form of currency so safe is the fact that the ledgers are accessible to users. These users constantly cross-check the ledgers, which makes it incredibly difficult for a hacker to alter any part of the blockchain because any changes stand out against all of the copies in the network. Each transaction is transparent, and with so many people constantly checking and working together, any attempts at hacking are quickly spotted. Because of its security, block-chain transactions are incredibly quick as they do not need to have long security check periods.

THE BLEEDING EDGE

Everyone knows what cutting-edge technology is—the latest and greatest, the most advanced and innovative technology. Bleeding edge is something even newer that cutting edge; it's technology that is so new it's still considered a risk. Bleeding-edge technology could change the world, or it could fail and disappear. These types of technologies are so radical and unique, it takes time for people to understand them, and education is scarce because even experts are still learning how they work and how they can best be utilized. It can take several years for the technology to improve and be utilized by the public.

Cryptocurrency is a technology that was recently considered bleeding edge. Taking the world by storm, it experienced a bubble in 2013 where the price of bitcoins skyrocketed and were at their peak worth $1000 per coin. This was considered a hype cycle, or a short period of time when the technology was in a rapidly growing bubble where people were excited and taking part.

Within the last few years, bitcoin has settled and is no longer growing as quickly as it did when it was considered bleeding edge. However, the technology is still new, and jobs are still being discovered in this field. Always consider the pros and cons of entering a field that is new and still evolving, versus a field that is more established.

HOW TO BECOME A CRYPTOCURRENCY DEVELOPER

Cryptocurrencies and blockchain is such a new and open technology that it's easy to find educational resources. Videos, articles, and papers are all available for free for anyone to watch, read, and gain a better understanding. Books and online courses are also available, with some courses being sponsored by large companies and Ivy League colleges.

Developers should have an understanding of how the entire cryptocurrency system works. They can do this by signing up and purchasing some cryptocurrency and using it for transactions. Cryptocurrencies like Bitcoin have pages that explain how they work, allowing anyone to learn about its cryptocurrency and its different uses.

Because blockchain and cryptocurrencies are just being implemented and explored by larger companies, someone interested in the industry needs to have a firm grasp of traditional coding and software building. This is because blockchain is often integrated into existing technologies and services, and newer products will need to be built upon common frameworks. So people interested in cryptocurrencies aren't just learning about blockchain, they're also learning multiple coding languages to bring blockchain to the rest of the tech world.

After learning coding and reading and understanding blockchain, reaching out to a cryptocurrency community is important. With cryptocurrencies so transparent and being made up of a network of people, these communities are a wealth of information to anyone interested in learning. Communities share knowledge and solve problems, allowing you to learn through your peers as you experiment with cryptocurrencies. These are also places where people will come together to work on projects. Joining a project will help you gain experience with working on a team as well as solving problems that arise with cryptocurrencies.

PROSPECTS AND PAY FOR CRYPTOCURRENCY DEVELOPERS

Cryptocurrency is currently a cutting-edge technology. This means that it's being explored by large companies but hasn't become fully integrated. Because it's so new, companies are testing and inventing to see how they can best use this technology and there are very few experts. As cryptocurrency continues to grow in popularity and be used by more companies, so will the demand for developers. Developers can expect to find salaries that are competitive in order to attract a short supply of workers.

Cryptocurrencies are a complicated and new technology, so people interested in a career should be people who

You can meet up with other people interested in cryptocurrency through clubs or groups that hold events or gatherings, either in person or online.

enjoy learning not only coding but also studying the financial world. People who enjoy solving complex problems and dreaming up new uses for technologies may be a good fit for developing cryptocurrencies, as the industry itself is rapidly evolving and taking shape. The fast paced growth of the industry should be taken into consideration as practices, regulations, standards, and other guidelines are still being discussed and developed.

FOR MORE INFORMATION

ORGANIZATIONS

American Statistical Association
732 North Washington Street
Alexandria, VA 22314-1943
(703) 684-1221
Website: http://www.amstat.org
Founded in 1839, ASA is the world's largest community
   of statisticians. ASA supports the development,
   application, and dissemination of statistical science.

Cryptocurrency Standards Association
NYDesigns
45-50 30th Street, Suite 9
Long Island City, NY 11101
(718) 663-8463
Website: http://www.crypsa.org
This organization focuses on stabilizing the bitcoin
   industry and creating a series of standards.

IEEE Computer Society
2001 L Street NW, Suite 700
Washington, DC 20036-4928
(202) 371-0101

Website: https://www.computer.org/web/guest
IEEE Computer Society provides resources, conferences,
    journals, and a digital library for those interested in
    computer science and technology.

BOOKS

Antonopoulos, Andreas M. *Mastering Bitcoin: Unlocking
    Digital Cryptocurrencies.* Sebastopol, CA: O'Reilly
    Media, 2014.
Narayanan, Arvind. *Bitcoin and Cryptocurrency
    Technologies: A Comprehensive Introduction.* Princeton,
    NJ: Princeton University Press, 2016.
Vigna, Paul. *The Age of Cryptocurrency: How Bitcoin and
    the Blockchain Are Challenging the Global Economic
    Order.* New York, NY: Picador, 2016.

BLOGS

Blockchain Technologies. "Cryptocurrency
    Explained: The Ultimate Guide to Understanding
    Cryptocurrency." 2016. http://www.
    blockchaintechnologies.com/blockchain-
    cryptocurrency.

Grothaus, Michael. "How to Create Your Own
    Cryptocurrency." Fast Company, 2014. https://www.
    fastcompany.com/3025700/how-to-create-your-own-
    cryptocurrency.
Hutt, Rosamund. "All You Need to Know About
    Blockchain, Explained Simply." World Economic
    Forum, 2016. https://www.weforum.org/
    agenda/2016/06/blockchain-explained-simply.

WEBSITES

Because of the changing nature of internet links, Rosen
Publishing has developed an online list of websites
related to the subject of this book. This site is updated
regularly. Please use this link to access the list:

http://www.rosenlinks.com/CCWC/coding

CHAPTER 11

PRODUCT MANAGEMENT

Product management is a role that oversees every stage of the product's life cycle. Product managers, sometimes called project managers, know how the developers are building the project, but they're also talking to marketing, testing, and watching the metrics. A product manager is an experienced builder, but also a business savvy team leader that knows the target market of the product and how to sell it. A product manager can not only take critique but give it in a way that is constructive to others. Every team reports to the project manager from each department and for each stage of the product. Product managers make sure the deadlines are met and any problems that arise are worked on and solved. They are the glue that holds the entire project together, and the people that speak on behalf of the product and the team.

All of the other careers in these sections can lead you to become a product manager; experience is the key.

HOW TO BECOME A PRODUCT MANAGER

Product managers make a higher than average salary. This is because they often have a lot of experience in one field or another before being hired for this job. This isn't an entry-level position, and while some companies may look for a higher education degree, like a master's, you can become a product manager without going to college. Small companies and startups in particular tend to care less about degrees and more about experience.

To be a product manager without a college degree, you need to have had experience elsewhere. You need to have worked on building multiple products. The jobs you have before you become a product manager don't have to be specific to management, but they have to show that you know

TECHNOLOGY, USER EXPERIENCE, AND BUSINESS SENSE

There are three areas of business a product manager needs to master; technology, user experience, and business sense. These are all very different, and while project managers may know one very well, they are expected to learn the others as they take on more of a leadership role.

For any project they manage, project managers need to have a working knowledge of the technology being created. They need to know some coding and understand the framework the product is being built on. This is so they can accurately and clearly communicate with the engineers working on the project. A good project manager knows what changes are being made and why, as well as what problems the team of engineers must solve.

Project managers also need to understand user experience, allowing them to talk to UX designers and testers to improve the customer-facing side of the product. Project managers understand the fundamentals of testing, design, and the value of the product to the user. In the end, the product will be in the users' hands, and the project managers should know what kind of experience the users need to have in order for the project to be successful. They are invested in how the users will interact with the product and its ease of usability.

Communicating these internal and external pieces of the project is essential. This means not only being able to communicate them but also to be able to explain the product's overall impact on business. This is where the third area, business sense, is needed. Project managers need to have a firm grasp of the business operations of the company and the market the product is a part of, and they need to be able to discuss it to others in the company, clients, partners, and users. Their business experience allows them to bring all of their knowledge forward and sell the project to everyone else.

how to work on a team. You could start out as an engineer where your understanding of technology could begin, or as a designer and bring your knowledge of user experience. There are many parts of a team you could be a part of before becoming a product manager: it all depends on what interests you.

Experience with working on products in teams should be supplemented with learning more about how to become a product manager. There are many books and online resources that discuss how to product manage successfully. Learning to speak in public is important, as a product manager has to communicate with everyone who is not working on the product. Someone interested in product

Product managers are needed everywhere. Tatsuo Nomura is the senior product manager for the smash-hit mobile game Pokemon GO.

management may want to take a class on public speaking or on how to write and improve communication skills. They may also want to take classes or read books on management, team building, and conflict resolution.

To gain experience as a project manager, look to meetups and events like hackathons. Leading a small team in a hackathon competition will help you grow as a product manager and practice the leadership and team skills you need during a very short time frame. You can also be the team member that stands up and sells your product to the judges, explaining to them what problem you wanted to solve, how you solved that problem with your product, and giving them a demonstration of the product. With every hackathon you join and compete in, the more you can add to your résumé to show your skills as a product manager.

PAY AND JOB PROSPECTS FOR PRODUCT MANAGERS

Product managers are needed for all sorts of projects. As our technology expands and grows, companies create more and more products to assist us in our everyday lives. Behind each product is a team, and leading each team is a product manager.

Remember that before you become a product manager, you'll need experience working on projects within teams. This career is more of a level up from other careers in this resource, and you will need to start as a developer or a designer and grow in that role and learn more skills before becoming a product manager. It may take a long time before you're able to become a product manager, so you need to be comfortable working that beginning job. The path to being a product manager can be longer than the other careers in this resource, so it's up to you to decide if this job is worth the time and patience.

FOR MORE INFORMATION

ORGANIZATIONS

Association for Project Management
Ibis House, Regent Park, Summerleys Road
Princes Risborough, Bucks HP27 9LE
United Kingdom
Website: http://www.apm.org.uk
This charity organization focuses on the placement
  of and advancement of project management.

Computer History Museum
1401 N Shoreline Boulevard
Mountain View, CA 94043
(650) 810-1010
Website: http://www.computerhistory.org
This nonprofit museum preserves the history as
  well as explores the impact of computing on
  the world.

Project Management Institute
14 Campus Boulevard
Newtown Square, PA 19073-3299
(855) 746-4849
Website: http://www.pmi.org

This organization focuses on the advancement of careers for people in project management roles.

BOOKS

Cagan, Marty. *Inspired: How to Create Products Customers Love.* Sunnyvale, CA: SVPG Press, 2016.

Haines, Steven. *The Product Manager's Survival Guide: Everything You Need to Know to Succeed as a Product Manager.* New York, NY: Mcgraw-Hill Education, 2013.

McDowell, Gayle Laakmann. *Cracking the PM Interview: How to Land a Product Manager Job in Technology.* New York, NY: Mcgraw-Hill Education, 2013.

BLOGS

Chu, Brandon. "PMs, You Don't Need That Technical Degree." 2014. https://medium.com/@brandonmchu/pms-you-dont-need-that-technical-degree-7d8fb196bccd#.gewomlbk0.

Walk, Hunter. "Ode to a Non-Technical Product Manager." 2012. https://hunterwalk. com/2012/08/18/ode-to-a-non-technical-product-manager.

WEBSITES

Because of the changing nature of internet links, Rosen Publishing has developed an online list of websites related to the subject of this book. This site is updated regularly. Please use this link to access the list:

http://www.rosenlinks.com/CCWC/coding

GLOSSARY

BACK END The systems that power a product. Servers, databases, and applications that keep everything running smoothly.

BLEEDING EDGE Technology that is so new it's still developing and considered risky.

BLOCKCHAIN The decentralized security technology behind cryptocurrencies that operates on a network of users.

CRUNCH A period of time when a deadline for a product is near and employees are expected to work overtime, often without overtime pay.

CRYPTOCURRENCY A secure system of digital transactions protected by a security technology called blockchain.

CUTTING EDGE Advanced and innovative technology.

DATA ANALYST A person who takes data and cleans, processes, and breaks in into small, digestible forms. Data analyzation is about the exploration of data.

DATA SCIENTIST A person who focuses on taking data and explaining the past, problem solving the present, and strategizing the future.

DEVELOPER/ENGINEER A person who creates and builds software and programs.

DEVOPS Development operations.

FRONT END The portion of a product that the customer interacts with.

FULL STACK Both the front end and the back end of a product.

HYPE CYCLE A period of rapid expansion and growth in users and popularity; a more extreme version of a bubble period.

IOS Apple's mobile operating system.

MACHINE LEARNING The ability for a computer to learn without being programmed to do so.

NEURAL NETWORKS A certain type of machine learning that is designed to mimic the neural network of the brain.

PRODUCT LIFE CYCLE The stages of a product's build from start to finish.

SYS ADMIN System administrator.

UX User experience.

BIBLIOGRAPHY

Albright, Dan. "How to Become a Data Scientist." MakeUseOf, March 6, 2015. Retrieved November 21, 2016. http://www.makeuseof.com/tag/become-data-scientist.

"Must Read Books for Beginners on Machine Learning and Artificial Intelligence." *Analytics Vidhya*, October 1, 2016. Retrieved October 16, 2016. https://www.analyticsvidhya.com/blog/2015/10/read-books-for-beginners-machine-learning-artificial-intelligence/.

Cooper, Michael W. "7 Critical Skills for QA Testing Career Survival." *TechBeacon*, October 31, 2016. Web. Retrieved November 1, 2016. https://techbeacon.com/7-soft-skills-every-qa-tester-needs.

Donnelly, Jacob. "Here's What the Future of Bitcoin Looks like—and It's bright." *Venture Beat*, February 14, 2016. Retrieved November 30, 2016. http://venturebeat.com/2016/02/14/heres-what-the-future-of-bitcoin-looks-like-and-its-bright/.

Finley, Klint. "The Modern Data Nerd Isn't as Nerdy as You Think." *Wired*. Conde Nast, November 4, 2013. Web. Retrieved September 15, 2016. https://www.wired.com/2013/04/phd-data-scientist/.

Francis, William J. "So You Want to Be an Android Developer? Start with These Resources." TechRepublic

July 31, 2015. Retrieved October 3, 2016. http://www.
techrepublic.com/article/so-you-want-to-be-an-
android-developer-start-with-these-resources/.

Golson, Jordan. "Apple's App Store Now Has over 2
Million Apps." The Verge. The Verge, June 13, 2016.
Retrieved September 30, 2016 .http://www.theverge.
com/2016/6/13/11922926/apple-apps-2-million-
wwdc-2016.

Ivins, Jessica. "My Advice for Becoming a UX Designer."
Jessica Ivins. Jessica Ivins, May 27, 2014. Retrieved
October 3, 2016. http://jessicaivins.net/my-advice-for-
becoming-a-ux-designer/.

Magain, Matthew. "How To Get Started In UX Design – UX
Mastery." UX Mastery. UX Mastery, March 16, 2016.
Retrieved September 15, 2016. http://uxmastery.com/
how-to-get-started-in-ux-design/.

Na. "Do You Need a Degree to Be a Game Designer?"
Video Game Designers. Game Designing, October
5, 2016. Retrieved October 12, 2016. http://www.
gamedesigning.org/career/do-you-need-college/.

Norma, Lindsay. "How to Become a UX/UI Designer When
You Know Nothing." LinkedIn. LinkedIn, July 2, 2014.
Retrieved September 15, 2016 https://www.linkedin.

com/pulse/20140702131658-43610144-how-to-
become-a-ux-ui-designer-without-design-school.

Rayej, Shima. "How Do Self-driving Cars Work?" Robohub.
June 3, 2014. Retrieved September 30, 2016. http://
robohub.org/how-do-self-driving-cars-work/.

Reillr, Brendan. "Common Tasks for a Storage
Administrator." SearchStorage. Tech Target. Retrieved
October 30, 2016. http://searchstorage.techtarget.com/
answer/Common-tasks-for-a-storage-administrator.

Schreier, Jason. "The Horrible World Of Video Game
Crunch." Kotaku. Gawker Media, September 26,
2016. Retrieved October 3, 2016. http://kotaku.com/
crunch-time-why-game-developers-work-such-insane-
hours-1704744577.

Stuart, Keith. "How to Get into the Games Industry – an
Insiders' Guide." The Guardian. Guardian News and
Media, March 20, 2014. Retrieved September 15, 2016.
https://www.theguardian.com/technology/2014/
mar/20/how-to-get-into-the-games-industry-an-
insiders-guide.

Watkins, Christopher. "7 Skills You Need to Be an IOS
Developer." Udacity, March 5, 2016. Retrieved October
12, 2016. http://blog.udacity.com/2016/02/7-skills-you-
need-to-be-an-ios-developer.html.

INDEX

ABOUT THE AUTHOR

Asher Powell is a proud nerd and former tech industry professional who has previously worked in Silicon Valley as a social media marketer. He has attended a hackathon and listened to startup pitches over coffee. Now a writer, he enjoys telling stories and learning about the future of technology with his very fluffy cat by his side.

PHOTO CREDITS